TABLE OF CONTENTS

JOB READINESS HAND BOOK

Eashwar N. Rathod B.

M.B.A., M.A. [Eng. Lit.]

Assistant Professor And

Soft Skills & Linguistic Skills Trainer

At Kalasalingam Group Of Institutions.

&

Prof. Dr. A. Alavudeen

PH.D., M.E., B.E.

Professor And Director Corporate Relations

At Kalasalingam University.

Invincible Publishers

First published in India in 2019

ISBN: 978-93-88333-86-3

Registered Address: 201A, SAS Tower, Sector 38,
Gurgaon-122003

Printed at Thomson Press (India) LTD

PREFACE

The evolution of this book has been inspired by a quote, "*The problem with India is not Unemployment but it is Unemployability,*" by India's greatest sons of all time, who is also famously called as "The Missile Man of India," DR. APJ ABDUL KALAM. Dr. Kalam always insisted that people, especially academicians, should give something back to the society. As a small and humble gesture we have decided to give something back to the society in the form of this book.

This book is all about the skill set, also known as employability skills, that is needed by a job seeker to prosper in his/her career. This book speaks about being motivated; setting goals; speaking in English without grammatical mistakes; enhancing one's soft skills - communication, teamwork, leadership, being flexible, problem solving, strengthening interpersonal skills, to manage time aptly; business communication - reading comprehension, email writing, essay writing, letter writing; self-introduction; how to speak instantly - extempore/impromptu/free-speech; how to speak effectively during JAM sessions; improve telephone manners; how to groom - dress and appear professionally; how to carry a positive body language to a successful career; how to be effective during a group discussion; tips to build an impressive CV / Resume; tips to clear an interview successfully with ease; and finally an assessment sheet on the topics that have been discussed in the book.

IN MEMORIAM

As This Effort Of Ours Was Possible Only With The Guidance And Path Shown By The Ultimate Power, Irrespective Of The Name That One Chooses To Call, We Dedicate This Book To **The Almighty God.**

CHAPTER 1

MOTIVATION STORIES

Ms. Gomathi Marimuthu Wins Gold Medal

An ex-student of Velammal Vidyalaya, in the village of Mudikandam in Trichy, was **Gomathi Marimuthu**. She was welcomed with an outpouring of wishes from the school children, local residents, as well as her former teachers after many years and also after the achievement, at the age of 30 years, of conquering the 800 meters race in Doha, Qatar. She spoke to a leading magazine and mentioned, "*I have become quite emotional after attending my felicitation programme in my own school. I have advised the youngsters that nothing is impossible if one has the determination and grit like I had.*"

Hailing from a very poor family, Gomathi recollects her father, Marimuthu, who was a daily wage farmer, working in the fields. She said, "*My father passed away three years back in 2016. He used to wake me up at 4 AM every day and forced me to wake up as well to go for running. I used to take part in more or less all the games, during my school days, but I always had an inclination towards athletics. Hence, I started practicing seriously post graduating to college under my coach Gandhi."*

Gloomily for Gomathi, she lost both her father and her coach the same year. Reminiscing the past she said, "*My mother, Rasathi, had to go out of home to work in the same fields where my father used farm. She wasn't able to do all the work by herself and hence, I used to assist her.*"

Fate had shown her ugly face to Gomathi once again, this time in the form or a groin injury. This injury has forced her to pull out of the competitions in 2016 and take complete rest. Despite the medical advice given by the doctors, she had to help her mother in the fields and sometimes in the scorching sun.

"I was inspired by Shiny Wilson"

Gomathi said that there were two factors that have revitalized her depression, because of which she was at the verge of quitting her athletic career. The first factor was her friend, Francis Mary by name. Gomathi was unable to cope up with the proper running shoes and also good diet to get stamina. "*I used to run on barefoot during my training sessions, usually held after my college, as I couldn't afford. I couldn't even arrange for proper diet because of lack of finances."*

The second and most important factor was **Shiny Wilson**. She described, *"Many of our coaches and teachers used to tell us the story of Shiny madam's struggles and how she overcame those ordeals to become one of India's best athletes. These dossiers were given to us during our training days, college meets, district and state meets. In fact her story had really inspired and motivated me to be back on track in 2017."*

Dr. APJ Abdul Kalam

The Care of a Leader

While working a pivotal project with very high workload, one of the 70 scientists working under Dr. Kalam, requested permission to leave by 5.30 PM, on a particular day, to take his kids to the exhibition. Dr. Kalam granted him the permission but to his dismay the scientist had forgotten the promise made to his kids and got engrossed in his work. By the time he realized, the time was 8.30 PM and he hurried to see Dr. Kalam to inform. Unable to find his boss, the scientist got disappointed that he couldn't fulfill his promise made to his kids went home with a burdened heart. Upon reaching his home he couldn't find his kids at home and queried his wife about them. *"Don't you know? Your manager came here at 5.15 PM and took the*

children to the exhibition," she said. The observation of Dr. Kalam has been so precise that finding his dedicated scientist engrossed in work, he took the responsibility of his kids.

Dr. Kalam Invited Two Special Guests as Presidential Guests

The President has the privilege to invite any two people as the "Presidential Guests" to the Raj Bhavan of any state and Dr. Kalam exercised this right during his first visit to Trivandrum. He had spent a great amount of time, as a scientist, in Trivandrum. One would be surprised by the kind gesture of Dr. Kalam's guests at the Raj Bhavan in Trivandrum. One was a roadside cobbler who was quite close to him during his time in Kerala; and the owner of a very small hotel where he used to have his meals.

The Man of Ethics (against acceptance of favors or gifts)

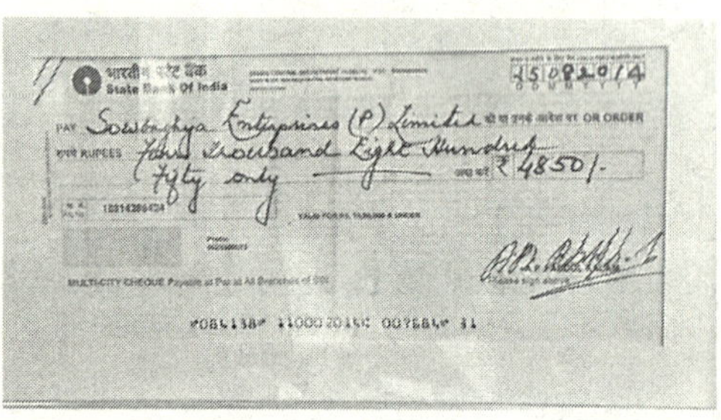

State Bank Of India
25 08 2014
PAY Sowbhagya Enterprises (P) Limited OR ORDER
RUPEES Four Thousand Eight Hundred Fifty only ₹ 4850/-

Once, Dr. Kalam was invited to a program in Erode, which was sponsored by Sowbhagya wet-grinders. He was gifted a wet-grinder by the sponsors. He, however, refused to accept it but since he had a need for it, he insisted on paying for it. He sent a cheque for Rs. 4850/- dated August 25, 2014 to the shop.

The Managing Director of the company didn't want to take money from Dr. Kalam and hence did not encash the cheque for over a month. After a month, they received a call from Dr. Kalam's office seeking an explanation for not depositing the cheque. In fact Dr. Kalam has directed them to deposit the cheque failing which he would return the grinder. The company, finally, has agreed to deposit it. However, they wanted to have a memorabilia of the cheque and have decided to keep a copy of the cheque. Hence they have got it scanned and have framed it as well. The following day they have deposited the cheque and have received a "thank you" message from Dr. Kalam's office.

Leadership Qualities of Dr. APJ Abdul Kalam:

Everything is possible: Dr. Abdul Kalam, Former President of India, was the son of a small boat owner, from far end of the country reaching, what was possibly, the supreme most position, a Citizen of India can ever reach and that too only one out of a billion people who could ever reach once in 5 years with a lot of hard work, dedication and sincerity which were backed by destiny.

Leaders motivate and ignite others to succeed:

Dr. Kalam was a destiny's child. A man with nothing except curiosity and passion for flying, with wings of fire, he flew as high as he could in the sky. Like an exceptional satellite that orbits the universe, he went about his mission of life, igniting millions of young minds in many nations.

Leaders are those who care, share and are transparent:

Dr. Kalam boasted nothing but learnt as much as he can till his last breath. He kept nothing to himself but shared with transparency and sincerity to each and every one as he learnt everything from them till his last breath at IIM, Shillong.

Humble and Selfless:

Dr. Abdul Kalam's accession to the top post and possession of power was just one of those occasions which make him as humble as possible, so that the people who met him can feel stronger and humongous persona in their heart and life.

Leaders inspire, in fact, others and make them dream rather than making them live in their own dreams, and so did Dr. Kalam who inspired millions of young hearts to dream and made them to believe in their dreams. He wanted people to dream and to transform their dreams into thoughts that can result into actions. Dr. Kalam envisioned a developed India, which is very much a reality, through strong vision.

Humbleness – The Best Quality of a True Leader is what the truth is and Dr. Kalam strongly believed that future India's success rests over PURA (Providing Urban Amenities in rural areas) and that is the way forward, to create a developed India.

Leaders look for solutions to a problem with innovative mindset, and he cross-pollinated the idea of using the high-grade steel used in missile that can kill people and designed and developed, what is famously known as Kalam-Raju Stent – that now saves people which comes at a fraction of a cost when compared to those expensive ones thus making it more affordable. Dr. Kalam's idea of using the composite materials, which is used in missile frames, to make lightweight calipers.

Leaders create institution and they live as an institution personally. So was Dr. Abdul Kalam, who definitely was an institution. Blessed are those who are into teaching profession. For how much he loved teaching is known to the world. **Kalam Aiyya Institution** illustrates various departments such as Department of compassion, Department of positive energy, Department of dream, Department of mission and vision, Department of curiosity, Department of giving back to society and Department of Igniting Minds.

Mahendra Singh Dhoni

It is said that leaders are born and not made. But, watching cricketer Mahendra Singh Dhoni's career, one wonders if it was only luck or if he was following a management path or theory? His qualities as a leader and manager have been dissected, debated and discussed by sports journalists and management gurus in a similar way.

Is Dhoni a good leader because he possesses leadership traits and attributes or does he leverage these skills via major management theories to get the better out of himself and the team? I have tried to explore MS Dhoni's actions under the ambit of management theories like Emotional Intelligence, Collaborative Management Theory and Situational Leadership.

Emotional Intelligence

Emotional intelligence (EI) is the ability to understand and manage your own emotions, and those of the people around you. For leaders, having emotional intelligence is essential for success. After all, who is more likely to succeed - a leader who shouts at his team when he's under stress, or a leader who stays in control and calmly assesses the situation?

According to a renowned psychologist, there are five main elements of emotional intelligence: Self-awareness, Self-regulation, Motivation, Empathy and Social skills. The better you manage, as a leader, each of these areas the higher your emotional intelligence the better persona you possess.

Self-awareness:

Is Dhoni self-aware? Absolutely, I would say. You have to be aware of your strengths and weaknesses to catapult yourself from a small town to the team captain of the Indian cricket team. Dhoni's ability to shield himself and his team from superfluous influences in order to focus on the game is one of his biggest assets. MSD manages his emotions well, keeps his cards close to his chest. He knows, no matter what the situation is, he can always choose how to react to it. When things get tough, all eyes turn to the leader. And if the leader is composed and calm, it lends a great strength and hope to the team. And it also gets the opposition joggled.

Self-regulation:

"Leaders who regulate themselves effectively rarely verbally attack others, make rushed or emotional decisions and stereotype people compromise their values. Self-regulation is all about staying in control." This is the best way to sum up Dhoni. This element of emotional intelligence also covers a leader's flexibility and commitment to personal accountability. Dhoni is composed, equally calm in success and failure alike. Dhoni has often said that he doesn't believe in dwelling in the past, or living for the future. Rather, he gives the best he can in the present. He is proficient at handling criticism and praise. He is accountable, accepts and owns up to the mistakes publicly – as a player and as a team.

Rarely has Dhoni lashed out on his team in public, a tactic which was far too common in the past with many leaders. Captains, coaches and even players used media as a communication tool to criticize each other. This self-regulation has lead Dhoni to be a well-respected captain, even by senior players like Dravid and Tendulkar.

Motivation

A self-motivated leader works consistently toward his goals has extremely high standards for work. Here, motivation comes from within and is more positive when you compare it to extraneous factors that affect your motivation. Dhoni's locus of control is very internal. He is not blinded by the glamour and money. He plays the game for the passion towards the game. He competes with only himself and none other.

Empathy:

Leaders with empathy have the ability to put themselves in someone else's situation. They help develop the people on their team, challenge others who are acting unethically, give productive feedback and listen to those who need it. Many still hold dear memories of watching Dhoni letting Ganguly captain the side for a little during his last Test match. Or when he took to the sides, as team India took Tendulkar on their shoulders during the World Cup 2011 victory lap. He is also sympathetic towards bad performances, and supports players through their ups and downs. In Dhoni's words "We should also believe in the ones who failed in the team. At crucial times, a team member who was not able to deliver might do miracles".

Social skills:

Leaders who do well in the social skills element of emotional intelligence are great communicators. Leaders who have good social skills are also good at managing change and resolving conflicts diplomatically. They set an example with their own behavior. Since he became captain in 2007, Dhoni has used his networking and social skills to garner respect from his team members, seniors and juniors alike. He gives and gets respect.

Situational Leadership Theories

By looking at famous leadership styles, you can see that situational leadership follows the same styles as the behavioral theories. Dhoni's management style, mostly, trails the same theory. During a One-Day match recently, between India and Australia, bowler Ishant Sharma gave away 30 runs in an over at the fag-end, virtually handing over the game to the opposition. Dhoni pointed out that at the international level, he doesn't believe in guiding the bowler at every stage. "Individuals will have to own up; you have to rely on your positive traits. You can't spoon-feed bowlers at the international level. I think the last few overs were disappointing. It is an area of concern and it is getting worse."

MS Dhoni and Collaborative Leadership Theory

Collaborative Leadership describes an evolving body of theory and management practice, which is focused on the leadership skills and traits needed to deliver results across functional and organizational boundaries. In Collaborative Leadership, from the premise that "...if you bring the appropriate people together in productive ways with good information, they will create genuine visions and tactics for addressing the shared concerns of the organization or community".

Mohammed Azharuddin would always huddle with senior players during the drinks break and ask their advice on what to do next. Dhoni doesn't do that. When it comes to key strategic decisions, he is his own man, seldom seeking advice. And after losing a match, he doesn't need comforting.

It would appear like MS Dhoni would not be a great supporter of the collaborative leadership cause, as the turn-around time (TAT) on field to make decisions is very short. Hence, any change in strategy by Dhoni is usually not done in consensus with the senior players. Here, Dhoni's ability to give and keep space comes into the forefront.

Dhoni, intentionally or unknowingly, uses many management theories and styles in his captaincy. He has a better working understanding of these theories than most managers would, which has made him the best captain of the best Indian cricket team. To summarize I would say that Dhoni is the A-Z of Management Studies.

CHAPTER 2

GOAL SETTING

- **Goal** – One of the most important components to kick start one's life / career. Goal setting has to be done in the most strategic way. As an example, one can set his/her goal by always keeping plan b and plan c. In simple terms I would say that if I have planned to execute a particular work in one method, I would also think what if my method doesn't work out. That is why I would be ready with two alternate methods to complete the same task. This strategy is one of the best and also the most successful one as one is ready with the alternatives. Hence no additional time is required to prepare oneself.

A goal has to be SMART. SMART is defined as:

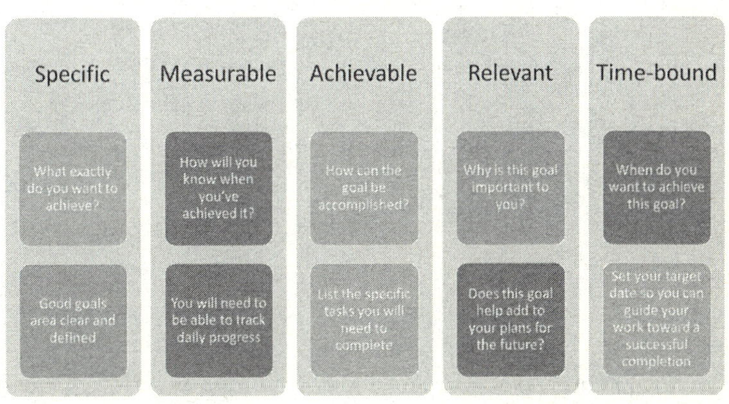

- **Specific** – A goal has to be specific rather than vague. E.g. I want to become an internationally famous Linguistic & Soft Skills Trainer. To achieve this goal I have done certifications such as TESOL and Voice & Accent from renowned institutions. Based on these certifications I got into the specific field of work and strived towards my goal. Today, I am proud to say that I am a guest faculty at 4 international universities where I take up English Communication Enhancement lectures and also Accent Neutralization lectures.

- **Measurable** – A goal has to have a measuring yard. E.g. I wanted to publish a book on Job Readiness. So if I don't set aside some time every day to do, I cannot do all the work in a day or two. We need to have to complete little bit of work every day so that you don't rush in the last moment.

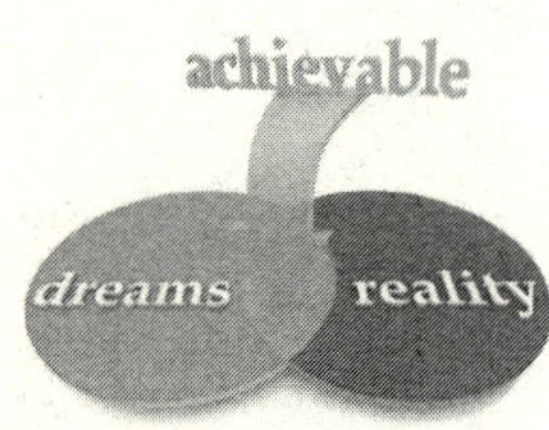

- **Achievable / Attainable** – A goal has to be relevant and not fictitious. E.g. I want to buy a Mercedes car by this month end, is a fictitious goal. If my salary is INR 5,00,000/- per annum and if this is my goal, I would be a joke. The same goal could be redefined by saying that I want to buy a Mercedes car in 5 years and for that I would save an 'x' amount every month.

- **Relevant** – A goal has to be relevant to the skill set that you possess or the financial situation that you are in. E.g. My goal is to become the manager of a reputed multinational company whereas I am short tempered and also I don't mingle with my team much. Now, when I lack patience and ability to mingle with people, how is it possible for me to become a manger. One has to know his/her traits in and out first and then set their goal/s accordingly.

- **Timely / Time-Specific** – A goal becomes one only if it has a timeframe else it is a wish. E.g. I want to become have a bank balance of INR 10,00,000/- by the month end. Now, this could not be possible, at least legally. However, the same could be possible by acquiring some additional skills and get into a job with a better package. Later the saving part comes into the scene and hence the said goal is possible.

S M A R T Goal setting is thus considered as one of the most important aspects of an individual because it makes a career or breaks it. Proper planning and goal setting have to go hand-in-hand to make one's life successful.

CHAPTER 3

MOST COMMON GRAMMATICAL MISTAKES MADE

Why do we need grammar?

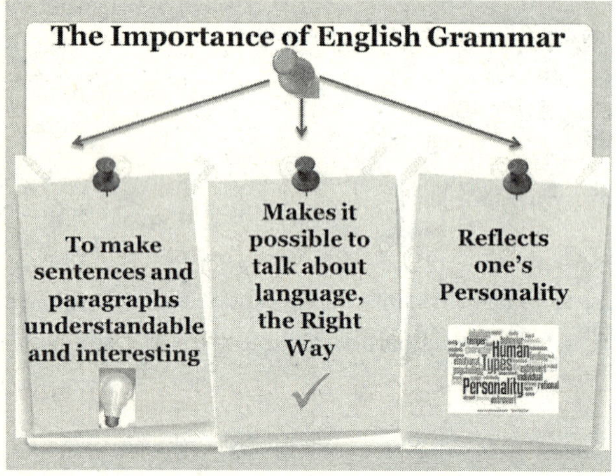

During my working days in the call centers, I used to be amused as how could the customer know that I am an Indian. Later, I understand that we as Indians have a specific way of speaking when compared to that of the native speakers. Most often it so happens that we tend to do a direct translation from our mother-tongue, commonly known as Mother-Tongue Influence or First Language Influence (MTI / FLI). We tend to form the sentences in our mother-tongue and then translate word to word. Now, the major issue in this situation is that the sentence structure of many Indian languages differs from that of English language. Hence there would many mistakes than we could ever imagine. Here are some tips that could, probably, assist one to use of tenses, prepositions and articles appropriately. The reason for me to choose tenses is that we make more number of mistakes in these areas.

- **Tenses** – We should understand that tenses depict the time of the action and hence the verbs have to be used accordingly. The simple way to get one's tenses right, is by understanding the use of each tense. Meaning, what tense is used in what situation. If one can get this understanding right, they would feel more confident in terms of sentence formation and thus public speaking becomes a cake walk. The usage of tenses is explained below, however not all the tenses are explained but only the ones that are used most are done so.

Tense	Usage	Rule/s	Sentence Structure
Simple Present Tense	Daily / Routine Activities, Traditions / Customs, Proverbs, Newspaper Headlines, Exclamatory sentences, Universal Truths, Habitual Activities, True / Declarative sentences and Explanation of a process or procedure	If the sub. is 3rd person singular i.e. He / She / It / Any singular noun, we add "s / es" to the verb. "Do" is used with I, We, You, They or Any Plural Noun. "Does" is used with He, She, It or Any Singular Noun.	+ve Sentence: Sub. + V_1 + Obj. -ve Sentence: Sub. + Do/Does + Not + V_1 + Obj. ? Form: Do/Does + Sub. + V_1 + Obj.?

Present Continuous Tense	An action is going on or happening right now	Never used for nouns of sense, feeling, thinking and possession.	+ve Sentence: Sub. + Am/Is/Are + V_4 + Obj. -ve Sentence: Sub. + Am/Is/Are + Not + V_4 + Obj. ? Form: Am/Is/Are + Sub. + V_4 + Obj.?
Present Perfect Tense	An action has completed just now or at an unknown/ unspecified time	"Has" is used with He, She, It or any singular noun. "Have" is used with I, We, You, They or any plural noun. After "has / have" always use the V_3 form of the verb.	+ve Sentence: Sub. + Has/Have + V_3 + Obj. -ve Sentence: Sub. + Has/Have + V_3 + Not + Obj. ? Form: Has/Have + Sub. + V_3 + Obj.?

Present Perfect Continu-ous Tense	An action has start-ed sometime in the past and is still in progress upto now	To mention the "Timeframe" is very important in this tense as that would be the key for one to identify that the action started in the past.	+ve Sentence: Sub. + Has/Have + Been + V_4 + Obj. + Timeframe -ve Sentence: Sub. + Has/Have + Been + Not + V_4 + Obj. + Timeframe ? Form: Has/Have + Sub. + Been + V_4 + Obj. + Timeframe
Simple Past Tense	An action that com-pleted at a known / specific time	To mention the "Timeframe" is very important in this tense as that would be the key for one to identify that the action completed in the past. When we use "did" in a sentence, the next verb that comes is always a V_1 form. The rule says there can be only one V_2 form in a simple sentence.	+ve Sentence: Sub. + V_2 + Obj. + Timeframe -ve Sentence: Sub. + Did + Not + V_1 + Obj. + Time-frame ? Form: Did + Sub. + V_1 + Obj. + Timeframe?

Past Continuous Tense	a) When two actions were happening simultaneously in the past b) When a continuous action was interrupted by another action in the past	E.g. I was eating while brother was watching TV. The continuous action is written in past continuous and the interrupted action is written in simple past. E.g. When I was cutting an apple, I cut my finger accidentally. "Was" is used with I, He, She, It or any singular noun. "Were" is used with We, You, They or any plural noun.	+ve Sentence: Sub. + Was / Were + V_4 + Obj. -ve Sentence: Sub. + Was / Were + Not + V_4 + Obj. ? Form: Was / Were + Sub. + V_4 + Obj.?
Past Perfect Continuous Tense	When two completed actions which occurred one after the other in the past	The first completed action is written in Past Perfect whereas the second completed action is written in Simple Past. E.g. The patient had died before the doctor arrived. The house had burnt completely before the fire engines arrived.	+ve Sentence: Sub. + Had + V_3 + Obj. -ve Sentence: Sub. + Had + Not + V_3 + Obj. ? Form: Had + Sub. + V_3 + Obj.?

Simple Future Tense	An action that will happen in the future and also future planned actions	We can use "shall" or "will" before the verb, however "shall" depicts uncertainty whereas "will" depicts surety (in +ve and –ve sentences). "Shall" in the question form is considered as "seeking permission / suggesting". Hence we avoid using "Shall" in the question form unless you mean the same.	+ve Sentence: Sub. + Shall / Will + V_1 + Obj. +ve Sentence: Sub. + Shall / Will + Not + V_1 + Obj. ? Form: Will + Sub. + V_1 + Obj.?
Future Continu-ous Tense	An action which will be happening or be in progress some-time in the future	We can use "shall" or "will" before the verb, however "shall" depicts uncertainty whereas "will" depicts surety (in +ve and –ve sentences).	+ve Sentence: Sub. + Shall / Will + Be + V_4 + Obj. -ve Sentence: Sub. + Shall / Will + Not + V_4 + Obj. ? Form: Shall / Will + Sub. + V_4 + Obj.?

The other important factor to enhance English Language communication is to perform a mirror practice, also known as Self-Analysis Technique. One has to take up the challenge of public speaking as it causes inhibition, which ultimately leads to stage-fear. If one has to overcome the inhibition / stage-fear, mirror practice is the best tool to enhance self-confidence. Shoot a video of your mirror practice and watch it to know the areas of improvement and strengths. Then practice again with the corrections and shoot again. This practice could be performed till one becomes perfect and the best people to judge your performance and give you right opinion can be your friend/s, family members, teacher / trainer or siblings. The more the practice the better you can become.

Prepositions – Many times it has been observed that prepositions are used just by direct conversion from mother-tongue. Mentioned below are some of the prepositions which are often used wrongly. Some of them have been mentioned here with their meanings and apt usage for your benefit.

1. **Beside & Besides**

   Beside = By the side of, Next to, At the side of

   E.g.:We built a house *beside* the lake.

   Besides = In addition, More, Plus, Including

   E.g.:I speak English *besides* Telugu.

2. **Since & For**

   Since is used for Point of time

   E.g.:We have been here *since* 4 O' clock.

   For is used for Period of time

   E.g.:Smith stayed in that house *for* 4 years.

3. **Among & Between**

Among is used for more than two persons or things.

E.g.:They were quarrelling *among* themselves.

Between is used for two persons or things.

E.g.:There was an argument *between* the two girls.

4. **By & With**

By is used for an Agent

E.g.:Jane was murdered *by* her neighbor.

With is used for an instrument.

E.g.:I usually write *with* a ball-point pen.

5. **In & At**

In is used for larger places

E.g.:He was born *at* Zurich *in* Switzerland.

At is used for smaller places

E.g.:I lived *in* Brussels *at* Thompson Street.

6. **In & Into**

In is used with things or persons at rest position

E.g.:Jennifer was *in* the room.

He was admitted *in* the hospital.

Into is used with things or persons in motion

E.g.:We walked *into* the theatre.

Kathy got *into* the bus.

7. **On & Upon**

On is used with things or persons at rest.

E.g.:Lisa was *on* the dais.

Upon is used with things or persons in motion

E.g.:The cheetah pounced *upon* the deer.

8. **In & Within**

In = After the end of / At the end of

E.g.:I shall type he letters *in* two hours.

Within = Before the end of

E.g.:We shall complete the work *within* three months.

Articles – Another important aspect of English Grammar. The usage of articles has been another issue for many people. A gist of the usage of articles has been explained here.

"**A**", "**An**" and "**The**" are known as Articles. They are also known as demonstrative adjectives. Articles are of two types.

1. Indefinite Article: An article which does not refer to any particular person, animal or thing is known as Indefinite Article.

E.g.:'A' & 'An'

2. Definite Article: An article which refers to any particular person, animal or thing is known as Definite Article.

E.g.:'The'

"The" is used before:

- Names of Rivers / Seas / Oceans
- Names of Hills / Mountains
- Names of Gulfs
- Names of Groups of Islands
- Names of Famous Books (Including Religious / Holy books)
- Names of Historical Buildings
- Names of Newspapers & Magazines (Tabloids)
- Names of Certain Countries
- Names of Trains / Ships / Airplanes / Helicopters
- Names of Musical Instruments
- Nationalities / Communities / Sects
- Directions
- Superlative Degree Adjective
- Ordinals
- Adjectives when used as nouns

CHAPTER 4

SPOKEN ENGLISH ENHANCEMENT TIPS

English Language communication is a necessity now-a-days as most of companies need their prospective employees to speak good English. That is one of the reasons for the Spoken English institutes sprout like mushrooms in the market, currently. However, most of them are not justifying their role and are just minting money from the innocent students who are unaware of the right way to enhance their English language skills.

I came across many students who face this ordeal, in fact still come across, of improving English language skills. In this chapter we will get to find a solution to overcome this ordeal i.e. improving English speaking skills without anyone's help. If you have someone to speak with you in English, it is always a blessing. But it is okay even if you don't have anyone to speak in English with you. **One important point that we all should remember is,** "THERE IS NO SHORTCUT TO SUCCESS."

» **Think in English**

Most of the times speaking in a language isn't the difficult task. In fact it is how to think in the language. Majority of the people frame a sentence, they want to speak, in their native language (mother-tongue) and then translate it into English. This is the biggest blunder one can do to ruin their sentences. One needs to understand that the sentence structure of English differs from that of the others. Thus it forces one to use inappropriate grammar, tenses / articles / prepositions, etc. So if one has to communicate grammatically correct sentences the base is to start thinking in English. If this has to happen one needs to get a list of English verbs with meanings in regional language (for understanding and usage) and also the other tense forms - conjugate form (V1, V2, V3 and V4). Then the mirror practice should happen i.e. to start talking to the mirror, as if speaking to a friend, and start making simple sentences. This will encourage us to start speaking with others with ease as our self-confidence boosts up.

Many people have asked me as to what to speak with the mirror. One can be very creative and innovative while doing the mirror practice. E.g. one can describe things, describe incidents, explain a process like cooking biryani or how does a machine work. I used to make students explain their favorite subject to their peers or let them speak about the recently concluded technical seminar / fest or tell about their favorite picnic / tourist spot or their experience on their first day at college etc. The trick, to be effective in the mirror practice or speaking with friends, is to feel that situation or incident or imagine that machine is right in front of you and then speak. You would really be felt by your audience.

» **Get the flow / fluency by Listening to English News Channel**

Flow of thoughts is the primary objective at this point in time. One needs to focus on clearing the hurdles / obstacles that they are speaking rather than focusing on the grammatical errors that are being committed. Once the ride becomes smooth then grammar can be taken care of. Listen to English news channels. Don't listen to foreign news channels like CNN, BBC, etc. as the news readers are native speakers and it will be difficult for us understand them. Thus, listen to Indian news channels such as Times Now, Republic TV, NDTV 24x7, Mirror Now, CNN-IBN, etc. as we could become more confident and then we could switch to foreign news channels.

Understand the process of *listening* (your face towards the wall and not towards the TV) to English news channels. When we listen to a news channel our mind subconsciously grabs the verbiage / vocabulary and stores them. We will also enrich ourselves in comprehending (interpreting / understanding) the sentences spoken. Here again, don't expect that you can understand everything in one day. It is a process and will take at least 3 weeks to understand a complete 15 minute news program. The percentage of comprehending will increase day by day provided you spend at least 20 -30 minutes every day listening to the news channel. Upon practice we would start using the vocabulary, gained through listening to news channels, and would sound a bit more appropriate.

» **Tongue Twisters assistance**

Tongue twisters play an equally important role in enhancing the pronunciation of an individual. They can make our language sound more polished as the articulation (use of mouth organs to make a sound) would be better.

E.g. Betty bought some butter, but the butter was bitter. So Betty bought some more butter, to make the bitter butter better But the bitter butter made the better butter bitter. Don't trouble the trouble until the trouble troubles you If you trouble the trouble, the trouble will trouble you. She sells sea-shells on the sea shore.

» **Parroting / Repeating**

Finally, try to parrot the news reader i.e. read back whatever the news reader is reading. It will be pretty difficult in the beginning because by the time you start reading it back the other sentences will be missed. Don't worry about missing the sentences, just read whatever you could get to remember. Upon practice you will be able to read one or two complete sentences in a day or two. If one could achieve this feat, this will be the first step to success. Remember the more the practice the better the ability. Hence it is your zeal and interest to practice so that you could be right there on the path to success.

CHAPTER 5

SMART SOFT SKILLS

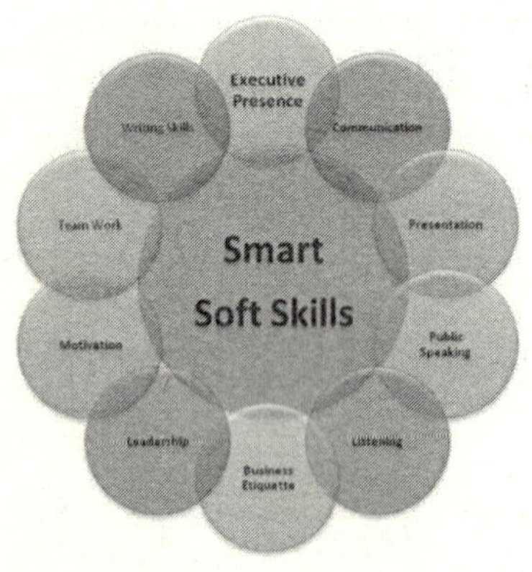

5.1 Communication – A good communicator is the one who is a good listener. In fact communication consists of 4 skills i.e. Listening, Speaking, Reading and Writing (LSRW). One who develops these skills can be a good communicator / orator. Communication skills include Presentation, Negotiation, Business Writing, Influencing, Selling skills and Teamwork.

5.2 Teamwork and Leadership – To complete certain work a team is needed and that is one of the reasons we have teams working in many corporates. Team – which stands for Together Everyone Achieves More – speaks for itself. Most of the teams have balanced aptly by the management.

However, sometimes the balance is inappropriate and it is then the responsibility of the team leader to make sure that the team is balanced. That is when the team looks for a guide. Now, who do you think will be a better guide for the team, a Boss or a Leader? I would say that the team definitely needs a Leader who can stand by the team, understand them, be there for them when needed, address their issues if needed, motivate them, provide them the space needed to perform, inculcate thinking out of the box techniques and lead them by examples. E.g. Mahendra Singh Dhoni – a true leader, a perfect analyst, a most trustable friend, an ideal mentor/guide and also a very approachable person to share one's feelings/opinions. These personality traits are something that a most successful leader, like MS Dhoni, should possess. Today, in the world of cricket, irrespective of their nationalities, MS Dhoni is one of the most respected personalities because of these wonderful and amazing personality traits, which indeed makes him one of the most successful Leaders/Captains in the cricketing world.

Likewise I would also like to talk about one of the books which has inspired and motivated me the most. This book has really made me, also many more like me, to rethink what our abilities are. It made many to go out and explore the opportunities that are waiting out there for them. I have read this book so many times and in fact I use many references from this book in my Soft Skills classes to many young professional students.

5.3 Flexibility/Adaptability – Flexibility / Adaptability can be defined as being ready to take up a responsibility when needed, even if it is beyond the work hours, and ensuring that the task is completed without being delayed. E.g. During my tenure in one of the corporate houses, on one particular day I have started the first shift. The second shift people were supposed to join so that I could end my shift and leave for the day. However, out of 4 people from the second shift only 1 person turned up and my team lead had asked me to continue the second shift as well. I told him that it would be difficult. He requested that the work flow is high and we may miss the SLA. Considering the team's performance and the request, a first time one, I have accepted and continued the second shift. It looked like I was being tested as the third shift teammates didn't turn up and I had to continue the third shift as well. I was drained out completely as I had covered a time window from 5 PM to 10 AM. My team lead has offered me additional 2 day-offs as compensation. I was later appreciated, in the form of a certificate, for my efforts. I was flexible enough considering the fact that work should not suffer and our team shouldn't be let down. In fact all my team members have the same kind of attitude and it is just because of the way our team lead handled and managed things with us, the rapport he maintained with us and his apt way of handling things.

Problem-Solving

1. Problem Identification
2. Problem Analysis
3. Plan Development
4. Plan Implementation
5. Plan Evaluation

5.4 Problem Solving – One of the key traits needed for any graduate, either experienced or inexperienced, to get employed. This trait focuses on the ability to analyze an issue / a problem, generate various ideas to resolve, evaluate those ideas and try to solve it in the most apt method / way. One should be ready to take up challenges and execute / finish them most satisfactorily at the same time adhering to the guidelines to be followed. The tip to excel / master problem solving is most probably by following the alternate plan i.e. if a problem can be resolved by implementing Plan A, we will go ahead. However what if Plan A fails, it is for us to be ready with Plan B and Plan C before implementing Plan A as it saves time. If Plan A fails then you already have Plan B and Plan C in place before hand and you can immediately implement them as well.

Plan A
Plan B
Plan C

5.5 Interpersonal Skills – We spend more time at the work place than our homes and hence it is advisable to keep the work place away from cheap and dirty politics. Day-in Day-out we meet each other, talk to each other and work together, thus it is better that our inter-relationships are clean and healthy. A successful employee can be the one with good relationship with colleagues and bosses and the key is to keep your personal life away from professional life as

troubles brew up if you mingle them. Wishing people, being polite, respect others, listening to their ideas/suggestions, keeping away our ego, keeping away from gossiping, willingness to learn rather than being rigid by saying that I know everything, being social / mingling with people, sharing the knowledge/work process, being able to assist others once you complete yours, in case of a conflict it is better that we sit and discuss to resolve the same, being flexible and maintaining a friendly attitude towards colleagues and bosses are some of the positive traits one could possess to be successful in maintaining a good rapport with colleagues.

5.6 Time Management – Managing time is one of the vital aspects of being an effective professional, which also makes an individual – both personally and professionally – well organized. There are certain tips, advised by the gurus of time management, that could make one an organized professional/individual.

- ✓ **Finish important tasks first**: The thumb rule of time management. To identify at least two or three most important tasks and completing them first, before taking up any other task, is one of the points to consider in time management.

- ✓ **Learn to say "No"**: An individual can be a good time manager if he/she can make a lot of time commitments if they know how to juggle through various engagements with ease. It would indeed be a great trait to possess. There is a risk in trying to enhance this trait as well. In the process of making many commitments one should also know to decline some of them based on the situation else it may be like one has taken a bite more than they can chew. Caution needs to be maintained and the ability to decline has to be enhanced as well.

- ✓ **Sleep of at least 7-8 hours**: If one thinks that working for an extra couple of hours could increase their productivity, they are wrong. To work effectively an individual needs at least 7-8 hours of sound sleep and if one is trying to wring a couple of hours from the working hours, it could have a negative on their productivity as well as health.

- ✓ **Devote your complete focus to the on-hand task**: Ensure to put your phone on silent mode and out of sight. Close all other bowsers to concentrate. If listening to music assists you to focus, it is better to do so. Immerse in yourself so that nothing comes between you and the work on-hand.

- ✓ **Start early**: If one is habituated to procrastinate / postpone his/her work, it would be better to ensure that the task on-hand is started early so that you don't rush, spending extra hours, towards the end. It is also advisable to organize oneself by allotting sometime every day and stick to it.

- ✓ **Don't get dragged down by unimportant details**: Certain projects often take much more time than expected, sometimes. If you are a perfectionist, it would be more difficult to complete the project as you tend to focus on too many minute details and get stuck with them. The key here is to continue to complete the said project and once done go for the revision at a later stage, else you would be stuck at the same point without any progress.

- ✓ **Transform key tasks into habits**: Writing is a passionate regular task of mine at college, work, leisure, etc. and I would probably write around 3000 - 5000 words per week. That is a lot to writing however I tend to manage it as it is a habit. I ensure that I write something every day for a long time. I ensure that I don't break this routine. My mind has got tuned to this habit thus it makes it easy for me to write because it is my passion.

- ✓ **Limit your time for TV/Internet/Gaming/Friends**: Spending time on TV, Internet, Gaming or Friends can drain up your time completely and hence it is advisable to fix up a schedule for these activities so that we could maintain our regular activities and on-hand tasks. This is possible by taking an analysis of the time being spent on these activities.

- ✓ **Demarcate a time limit to complete a task**: Preparing an action plan is a better idea before starting the task. It is suggested to plan like "I will be on this job until I complete this" would be wrong rather "I will be on this job for the next three hours" would be a better idea. Setting a time limit is always a better way to accomplish the tasks.

- ✓ **Do less:** This tactic has been recommended by one of my friends from the corporate world. He used to say that "slow down, understand what needs to be done first - prioritize and concentrate on those first." Do lesser things that reap more yields, rather than more things that are mostly void and null.

- ✓ **Utilize a little bit of weekends**: Most of the corporate employees curse and crib at their employers as they have been assigned tasks which need to spend their entire weekends. Ideally, it is inappropriate to do so as one has a personal life too and if you don't take care of it work life will suffer without saying. Weekends are meant to rejuvenate the upcoming week and if not taken care of the effect will show on the health as well. It is suggested to take up a little bit of your weekend and not the full one.

✓ **Create organizing systems**: Being organized makes one life much more easy by saving tons of time but at the same time it doesn't need one to be ultra/over organized as it makes life more complicated. E.g. creating filing system for documents, organizing all your files in appropriate folders on your computer, deleting unnecessary emails, etc., making sure that all the things are placed at apt places. Ensure that you unsubscribe yourself from unwanted mailing lists to avoid waste of time by organizing emails.

CHAPTER 6

READING COMPREHENSION, E-MAIL WRITING, ESSAY WRITING AND LETTER WRITING

6.1 Reading Comprehension:

Reading comprehension questions are generally designed to examine a wide range of abilities that are required to analyze one's reading skills.

Those abilities include:

- Understanding the meaning of individual words, sentences, paragraphs and larger text of bodies.
- Summarizing a passage and distinguishing between major and minor points in the paragraph.
- Drawing proper conclusions from the given information and reasoning from incomplete data to infer the missing information.
- Identifying the author's perspective and assumptions, analyzing a text and concluding about it.

- Identifying strengths and weaknesses of a position, developing and considering alternative explanations.

As the above list of abilities implies, reading and understanding a piece of comprehension or a piece of text requires a passive understanding of the content in the given paragraph. A comprehension consists of one to several passages and the questions may be asked from any of the passages in the given comprehension. The questions can cover the meaning of a particular word to assessing evidence that might support or weaken points made in the passage.

General advice to solve Reading comprehension

✓ Read and analyze the passage carefully before answering the questions.

✓ Pay attention to clues that help you understand less explicit aspects of the given passage.

✓ Distinguish main ideas from the supporting ideas as well as the one the author is advancing from those he or she is merely reporting.

✓ Distinguish hypothetical or speculative ideas that the author is strongly committed to.

✓ Identify the main transitions from one idea to another and the relationship between the ideas.

✓ Read each and every question carefully and be certain that you exactly understand what is being asked.

- ✓ Answer each of the questions based on the information provided in the passage and do not rely on the outside knowledge.

Reading Comprehension Assessment

Directions: Read the passage. Then answer the questions below.

Adam's family

April has a large family. She lives with four people. April also has two pets. April's mom is a doctor. April's mom helps people who are sick. April's dad works at home. He cooks for the family. April's dad drives the kids to soccer practice. April has two brothers. Eddy is ten years old and Bruno is fourteen years old. April has two pets. Milo is a small, black cat. Snoopy is a large, brown dog.

April loves her family. April's mom works at the hospital. She is very obedient to her mom and dad. Adam's brothers are quite indifferent and they are not like Adam. They act like strangers inside their home and they do not participate in any of the family activities. And due to the strange behaviour of her brothers, April gets disappointed very often.

Eddy is a passionate dancer since his childhood days. Bruno is a very good guitarist. Eddy and Bruno are not good in studies, but April is very good in her studies and she is the topper in her school. April always tries to earn good name to her parents. So she is very concerned about her discipline.

Questions :

1. How many people are in April's family?

   a) Four

   b) Five

   c) Six

2. April's mom works at the

   a) School

   b) Post office

   c) Hospital

3. This passage is mostly about April's

   a) Family

   b) Pets

   c) Soccer team

4. Which of the following is most likely true?

   a) April's mom coaches the soccer team

   b) Eddy is the best soccer player in the family

   c) Eddy and Bruno are part of April's family.

5. The oldest brother in April's family is

   a) Eddy

   b) Bruno

c) Milo

6. How is your family same as April's family? How is it different? Explain

Answers and Explanations:

1. B

Question Type: **Inference**

At the beginning of the passage, the author writes, "April has a large family. She lives with four people." If April is a person, and she lives with four persons and, we can tell that there must be five people in April's family. This means (b) is correct. The passage does not provide any information to support choices (a) or (c). Therefore they are incorrect.

2. C

Question Type: **Detail**

In paragraph 2, the author writes, "April's mom works at the hospital". This lets us know that April's mom works at the hospital. Therefore (c) is correct. The passage does not provide information to support choices (a) or (b). This means they are incorrect.

3. A

Question Type: **Global**

At the beginning of the passage, the author writes, "April has a large family." After this, the author describes the pets and the people in April's family. Using this information, we can tell that this passage is mostly about April's family. Therefore (a) is correct. The passage mentions April's pets Milo and Snoopy. They are a part of

Adam's family. The author spends more time writing about April's family in general. Using this information, we can tell that this passage is not mostly about April's pets. This means (b) is incorrect.

In next passage, the author mentions that the kids go to soccer practice. This is the only one detail in the passage. The author spends most of the time writing about April's family in general. Using this information, we can tell that this passage is not mostly about April's soccer team. Therefore option (c) is incorrect.

4. C

Question Type: **Inference**

At the end of the passage, the author writes, "April has two pets. Milo is a small, black cat. Snoopy is a large, brown dog." Right after this, the author writes, "Adam loves his family!" Because the author mentions April loving her family right after Milo and Snoopy are described, we can tell it is most like true that Milo and Snoopy are a part of April's family. This means (c) is correct. The passage does not provide information to support choices (a) or (b). Therefore they are incorrect.

5. B

Question Type: **Detail**

At the end of the first paragraph, the author writes, "April has two brothers. Eddy is ten years old. Bruno is fourteen years old." If Eddy is ten and Bruno is fourteen, we can tell the eldest brother is Bruno. This means (b) is correct. Eddy is younger than Bruno. Snoopy is a dog. Thus, the passage does not provide information to support choices (a) or (c), and they are incorrect.

6.2 Email Writing:

Email etiquette is as important as any other etiquette because the chances of being misunderstood are pretty high. Email writing is an art that could be mastered quite easily, but definitely with some practice and tips.

We would try to understand the key points that one needs to remember while writing an email.

✓ **Subject Line**

A subject should always summarize the message clearly and briefly.

E.g. Sub: Candidature for the position of an Assistant Professor – Reg.

Sub: Delay in shipment of order # AS12345 – Reg.

✓ **Short and Simple Sentences {SSS} or Keep It Short and Simple {KISS}**

Try to use crisp and short sentences. Using compound and complex sentences could force you to make grammatical errors. It is also observed that most of the people make the mistake of translating directly from their native language / mother-tongue to English, which is the root cause of grammatical errors. Hence we suggest an email writer to follow the SSS or KISS technique.

✓ **Consider the audience / reader**

Is the reader your boss, your client or your colleague? What kind of email do you want to write either formal or informal? A point to note here is that most of the corporate houses use a neutral tone in their emails. However, there are some points to note that make your email formal or informal.

Formal – Thank you for your enquiry seeking a quotation for Electric Scooter.

Informal – Thanks for your enquiry for a quotation of Electric Scooter.

Formal – I am afraid that I will not be able to make it

Informal – Sorry, I can't come

Formal – I was wondering if you could please assist me

Informal – Could you please assist me?

We may use informal emails to colleagues if they are friends as they are close to our speech and also that we could use conversational expressions and phraseology to express ourselves. Incorrect grammar could be acceptable in these emails. However, if the email is meant for a client or a senior executive in the company, incorrect grammar and informal phraseology will not be acceptable.

✓ **Apt usage of grammar, punctuation, spellings and capital letters**

The above mentioned points can be tolerated in an email however one needs to ensure that they are appropriate else the meaning of the email will change and also our image is tarnished. Always ensure that you make some time to edit, correct and check grammar and punctuation before sending the email. Remember to attach the files (that you want to send) first as you tend to forget towards the end (this is iterated as most of the times this is a blunder that many people tend to make).

✓ **Assess your speech, i.e. do you want to be direct or indirect, based on which you could frame your sentences.**

Direct – I need this job done in 1 hour.

Indirect – Could I have it on my desk in an hour?

Direct – I will be delayed.

Indirect – There would be a slight delay as my flight touched down late.

Direct – Your speech was awful.

Indirect – To be honest, your speech could have been better if it had .....

✓ **Maintain Optimism**

The choice of words one chooses depicts his/her personality. Hence it is ideal to be choosy while selecting one's words while corresponding. It is better to use words such as "I would be happy, I would be delighted, I would try to do my best, good query, mutual benefit, agree to, together, etc." rather than words such as "technical glitch, busy, failure, forget it, it is impossible, I can't, waste, hard, unsure, etc."

✓ **Try to measure your ability and enhance performance by getting feedback**

The best person to help you in this aspect could be your English language teacher / trainer. It could also be someone from your family or friends who are good at English, at least better than you.

One could start reading or going through emails written by other people. It is also better to start building vocabulary by observing the language and vocabulary used by others. You could also try finding synonyms of most of the words so that you could enhance your word bank.

6.3 Essay Writing:

There are many methods followed to write an essay. However, what I have learned as a kid is the 5 paragraph essay writing method, which has impressed me and also made my essays look pretty good. Let us know more about this method in-depth.

- Introduction Paragraph (this could also be the definition in some cases).
- Types (of the topic), if any (if no types are available then you could ignore this point.
- Causes (with examples to support your say/opinion).
- Demerits / Disadvantages (with examples to support your say/ opinion).
- Preventive measures and Conclusion (with examples to support your say/opinion).

Introduction paragraph / Definition

This paragraph could be used to define the topic and also mention some information about it, other than the causes and disadvantages about it.

Types (if any)

Here one can mention the different types available and explain them. Some topics may not have a definition and in such a situation we can ignore this paragraph.

Causes

This paragraph is where one can discuss the causes of the particular issue and provide supporting examples / data / statistics.

Demerits / Disadvantages

This paragraph is to explain the disadvantages or demerits of the topic with required statistics / examples.

Preventive Measures and Conclusion

This paragraph is the one where we can express the preventive measures that are needed to overcome the issue with required examples, of course. One can also mention their conclusion in this paragraph.

6.4 Letter Writing:

I have been an English Language Trainer, Soft Skills Trainer and a Linguistic Trainer for about 12 years. In my observation as a trainer I found out that most of the students either UG or PG are unable to write a letter. Ironic part of the situation is that some of the teachers / faculty members also cannot write a proper letter. Hence, I have chosen to include this topic as well in this section.

I have decided to include two formats of letters, one is formal letter and other is informal / casual letter.

Formal Letter

From:

Kevin Kent,

Flat # 225, Radiance Sunshine,

Kazhipattur, OMR,

Chennai.

10th May, 2019

To:

The HR Manager,

No. 36, Nu Central,

Job Street,

Kuala Lumpur,

Malaysia.

Sir/Madam

Sub - Candidature for the position of a Linguistic & Soft Skills Trainer - Reg.

With reference to your advertisement on your website, I would like to present my candidacy for the said position. My name is Kevin Kent. I am an Indian with 25 years of overall work experience. As a trainer, I possess 12 years of work experience. I hold two Master's degrees, one in English Literature and the other in Business Administration. I have been imparting employability skills to many students from professional colleges and universities globally. The pre-requisites of the job match at least 85% of the skill set that I possess. I am zealous with willingness to learn, punctuality, optimist and ability to mingle with people easily as additional traits.

Given an opportunity, I am sure that I could meet your expectations, if not exceed, and ensure the possibility of a mutual growth is set.

Yours sincerely,

Kevin Kent

Enclosure: My Curriculum Vitae.

Informal Letter

Kevin Kent,

Flat # 225, Radiance Sunshine,

Kazhipattur, OMR,

Chennai.

10th May, 2019

Dear Uncle Ben,

It has been a long time since I have heard from you. Hope that you and Aunt Laura are fine. Everyone back here is fine by the grace of god. I have got a job in one of the multinational companies in Kuala Lumpur, Malaysia. I would need your assistance to find a place to stay for me, as you are also placed in the same place. I will reach Kuala Lumpur on the 27th of May, 2019 and will let you know the flight details as soon as I get them.

Mom and Dad have conveyed their wishes to you and Aunt.

Yours Loving Nephew,

Kevin Kent.

CHAPTER 7

SELF-INTRODUCTION AND EXTEMPORE / IMPROMPTU / FREE-SPEECH & JAM

7.1 Self-Introduction

This has been a typical and most confusing question during my job seeking days. Many people have many versions of self-introduction. After working in many countries, I have come across many people introducing in many different ways. One should understand that each country has a different culture and mannerism that they tend to follow. However, the job scenario will always remain the same be it in the USA, Japan, Russia or India or to that matter any country. Hence what I believe is that one should ideally highlight their qualities in lieu to the pre-requisites of the job, their educational qualification/s, their achievements, family background (mention your father's profession, mother's profession and about your siblings), hobbies and interests. This is the format, which even I as a recruiter did look for; most of the HR personnel would look for in a candidate. As a just passed out graduand (means a graduate) never tell / use the phrase / word "fresher". The word "fresher" has / is considered in a different way all together. Instead of "fresher" one could always use other words such as "just passed out graduate", "inexperienced person", "do not possess any work experience", etc.

The following is a sample of a self-introduction at an interview.

Good morning sir/madam. As you are aware, my name is Ishwar Rathod (or) I am / My name is Kevin Kent. I possess a total work experience of 25 years - if you don't possess any work experience, you can say "I am a just passed-out graduate" or "I don't possess / have any work experience". I am an optimist possessing punctuality, flexibility, ability to mingle with others easily, reliability and jovialness as additional personality traits.

Talking about my achievements, I stood state first in my Hindi Pandit examination and also I was the youngest to do so from the state of Andhra Pradesh. A gold medal was conferred to me by the then governor Dr. Kumudh Ben Joshi. I have also stood state first in the type-writing high speed exam and was conferred with a gold medal by the Chairman & Managing Director of AP State Technical Education Board. I have been adjudged the best employee of the month for 11 consecutive months while working with GECFS. I have won the Annual Quiz Competition at HSBC, wherein around 300 employees have participated.

My educational qualifications are that I have completed my Master's degree in Business Administration from the University of Queensland, Australia and a Master's degree in English Literature from the University of Toronto, Canada.

My father was a manager in a cinema theatre. My mother was a teacher. I had a younger brother who used to work for a private bank *(the reason I used past tense to talk about my dad, mom and brother is that they have passed away).*

I love to listen to melodious songs mostly from Hindi, Telugu, Tamil and English languages. My interests include trying out different cuisines, whenever time permits, and watching cartoon movies.

Things not to do during Self-Intro:

- Avoid the use of beginning your introduction with "This is" or "Myself". "This" and "That" are ideally used before non-living things however since we are living beings it is grammatically incorrect to use them. Similarly, the usage of "Myself" as a subject is incorrect as it is not a subjective pronoun but it is a reflexive pronoun. Reflexive pronoun indicates that someone completed a work by themselves (without anyone's help). E.g. I have completed the job by myself.
- Avoid direct translation (from mother-tongue to English) as this will cause the sentence to be grammatically incorrect.

  E.g. I love listening songs - Incorrect.

  I love to listen to songs - Correct.

  I am going in a bike - Incorrect.

  I am going on a bike - Correct.

  I am travelling on a bus - Incorrect.

  I am travelling in a bus - Correct.

My favorite color is white, yellow, green and red – Incorrect.

My favorite colors are white, yellow, green and red – Correct.

- Try using simple sentences to converse, as it will be easy for you to speak and for the other to understand.

7.2 Free-Speech, Impromptu or Extempore

A speech given without any preparation or rehearsal is known as Extempore / Impromptu / Free-Speech. This round is one of the criteria in most of the interviews, as it exhibits the standard of the candidate to the recruiter. Similar to this round is the JAM round, wherein JAM refers to Just-A-Minute.

Let us look into the details of these rounds. Extempore (pronounced as ex-tem-pri or ex-tem-por) or Impromptu or Free-Speech is a speech where the candidate has to speak without any preparation / rehearsal. The topics given for this round are mostly social issues. However, sometimes the recruiters do give a minute time to prepare (optional). I would say that the trick here is to speak something similar to that of an essay. One should include certain elements to make the speech interesting and also to make you stand-out from the crowd. These elements could be:

(a) Definition or a couple of sentences about the topic (in case of non-availability of a definition)

(b) Causes

(c) Disadvantages / Cons

(d) Preventive Measures

(e) Conclusion

7.3 Jam

Though the motto of this round is the same as the above mentioned topics, but the process of JAM session or round is different from the above. JAM topics are generally situational and the topics given to speak are mostly controversial. Meaning, one should try to feel or be in that situation so that they could imagine and speak. One also needs to be smart while answering and ensure that the others do not get offended by our opinion. The best way to speak is to ensure that we are letting them know that we are speaking in general and have no intentions to hurt others' feelings. JAM topics can be cleared easily if one has the ability to imagine and speak in the flow. Description is the key to clear this round.

The criteria of selection in these rounds could be Language Skills, Confidence Level, Content, Flow of Thoughts and Body Language.

CHAPTER 8

TELEPHONE ETIQUETTE

Telephone – a very important invention in the life of human beings. It has reduced the distance between people though they are from different ends of the globe. It has been helping us to build businesses by means of quick communication and also to be empathetic and sympathetic. The apt way to answer a telephone could be done by following the following good practices for both incoming and outgoing calls.

➢ Identify yourself by telling your name and department / organization rather than just a "hello".

E.g.

- Thank you for calling ABC Pvt. Ltd. My name is Kevin Kent. How may I help you?
- Thank you for calling MBA department. I am Kevin speaking. How may I help you?
- Hello, my name is Kevin and I am from MyHome.com. May I speak with Ms. Julie?

- Good morning, I am Kevin from KK Publishing House. May I please speak with Mr. Ishwar Rathod?

- Your etiquette should remain the same, courteous and polite, towards people from both inside and outside the organization / institution.

- Ensure that you don't cross talk / interrupt (while they are speaking). Let the caller finish his or her sentence / idea / suggestion / query.

- If you couldn't get to speak with the person you called for, please don't inquire about his schedule.

  E.g.

- Oh! Is Mark not there? Could you tell me where is he?

- One should identify themselves even while answering the calls i.e. by your name, department, organization, etc.

- Always smile while answering the phone as your smile could be felt by the caller / listener. Remember that 55% of communication is done by non-verbal mode. We can feel if the person speaking over the phone is genuine, laughing, making fun, embarrassing, being sarcastic, etc. Hence be cautious while answering / making a call. Be happy.

- Be energetic and enthusiastic while answering / speaking over the phone. One should not sound monotonic or don't act while answering / speaking.

- While offering help try to sound genuine as your answer tells the speaker / listener as to what is on your mind. Rather acknowledge if you don't know the answer.
- It is always better to take down the name and the phone number of the caller before transferring the call, if needed. Also inform the caller that if the call gets dropped while transferring someone will call him/her back within some stipulated time.
- Be it a speaker or someone you call, we need to understand that both of them are either customer or client. Showing courtesy and respect at all times during the call will make them feel "I am an important person."
- Usage of respectful and considerate words and phrases, such as:

- "May I take a message?"
- "Would you like to leave your number?"
- "He's away from his desk. May I have him return your call?"
- "I'm sorry."
- "Thank you."
- "Please."
- "May I put you on hold?"
- "I'm sorry to keep you waiting."

- Don't use words and phrases, such as:
  - "Yeah / Yup."
  - "Huh?"
  - "She's at lunch. Call back later."
  - "I don't know where he is."
  - "I don't know where he is or when he'll be back."
  - "He's not here."
- It is a good practice to inform or explain the process that you are about to do, if not every time, at least most of the times such as: "May I place your call on hold while I try to get this information from the service department", "I may have to transfer this call to the service department as they would possess the complete data and to be on the safer side I would request you to kindly let me know your phone number and name so that if there is a call drop or call gets disconnected I can get back to you."
- Sometimes the names of the caller or client may be difficult to spell and/or pronounce, in such a situation it is always better to ask them to spell and/or pronounce so that they don't get offended by a wrong spelling or pronunciation. "Could you please spell your name for me, sir/madam." "Could you please pronounce your name for me, sir/madam."
- Sometimes the customer may be angry or rude. However, it is indeed our responsibility to empathize with them rather than you getting angry. It may be a situation where the caller may be

trying to speak to a human for a long time and couldn't get one or a caller may be facing a challenge or difficulty in solving the ordeal that they have been going through. So kindly empathize and let them speak. While the conversation goes on and you are empathizing continuously, you could notice that the caller's tone becomes softer after sometime. Sometimes they would even apologize for being rude. Give that humanly touch to your call and make the caller happy by providing a solution to their issue.

CHAPTER 9

GROOMING

Another key component of securing a job is grooming. As they say, "First impression is the last impression", it depends on the candidate as to what do they want. I would also call grooming as self-presentation. As an example, let us consider the scenario at a restaurant. When one walks into the restaurant, you see a cozy ambience where there is light music played in the background with dim lights. Once you order the food and it is being served you could observe that the food looks very attractive. It looks attractive because of the colors that they use i.e. White or Off-White crockery in which we have green gravy with red toppings or red gravy with green toppings. This makes the presentation of the food very attractive hence the phenomenon; "If your eyes like something, your heart automatically likes it" is proven.

Now, let us consider another situation. A friend of mine suggested me to try out the food at a roadside restaurant, also known as a dhaba, on the Chennai – Madurai highway as it is very yummy. I did go there to try it out but the master who came to take the order had his fingers, which were ugly and untidy, dipped in the water tumblers. The very look of that scenario itself killed my appetite. Hence I told him that I would come back in sometime and left the place. The food might have been very tasty however, the presentation is very bad.

Similarly, the way that we groom and present ourselves could make a lot of difference on the impact that we could make at the interview. The way a person dresses up for the interview gives an indication of his suitability for the job. Selection of wrong attire can be a turn off for the interviewers and may result in you losing the hard earned opportunity. To avoid such a scenario, let us gain a few insights for dressing up for an interview

Interview is an important part of the selection process. Even before you get a chance to showcase your skills, you have already been judged on the basis of your appearance and clothing. Both the male and the female candidates need to ensure that they dress up suitably for the occasion.

Attire for male candidates at an interview:

- The attire should be according to the environment and work culture.
- Dress-up should be appropriate and comfortable.
- Clothes need not be expensive but should be clean and well-ironed.
- A two piece matched suit is the best choice.
- Colors chosen may be black, navy blue and dark grey.
- If the suit is unaffordable, a light colored full sleeves shirt may be paired with dark color trousers.

- Either a blazer or a full sleeve sweater may be worn as part of the formal attire (optional).
- A plain tie goes with a suit or a shirt (optional).
- Avoid any shiny accessories.
- Dark colored socks of mid-calf length should be worn so that the skin is not visible while sitting.
- Formal shoes of black or brown color may be worn.
- Wear a belt that matches the color of the shoes.
- A big no to casual or sports shoes.
- Clean shaved or neatly trimmed beard.
- Don't carry too many things in your pockets.
- Never try a new look before an interview. It is better to take a hair-cut, preferably, a week prior to the interview.
- Male candidates, preferably, should wear a formal watch, if affordable.

Attire for female candidates at an interview:

- Female candidates should dress-up according to the culture and environment of the organization. Choose trousers paired with shirts with a formal blazer or a sweater. They may also opt for a saree or a suit.
- Dark-colored trousers, preferably, paired with a light colored formal shirt.

- The suit or the saree chosen should be simple without much embroidery or other work.
- Make-up should be little with light color lipstick or nail colors. The nails should be clean and well groomed. The interviewee should have her hair neatly tied up.
- Dark colored formal shoes should be paired with trousers.
- Wear flat or lightly heeled chappals with saree or salwar kameez.
- High heels are a big no.
- Shoes should not be open in the front.
- Don't apply too much of make-up.
- Don't wear heavy jewelry.
- The purse chosen should be simple and small. Don't carry a flashy purse. Black and brown colors should be preferred.

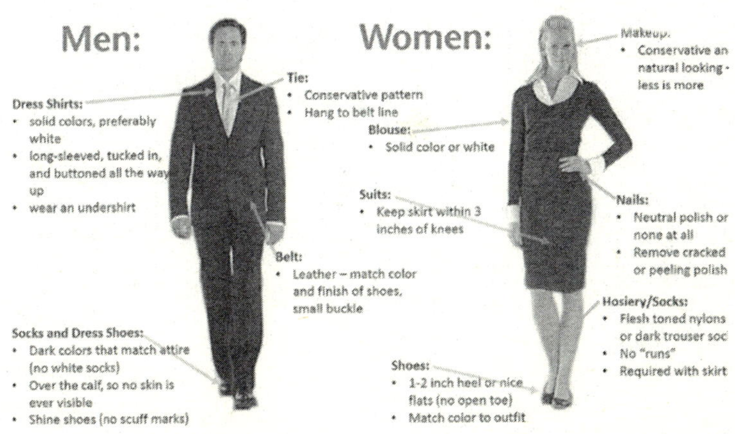

Confidence reflects in one's interview only if he/she feels so. So wear something that makes you comfortable and when comfortable automatically you would feel confident. If you adhere to these aspects, you could take care of the most important components of an interview i.e. The First Impression.

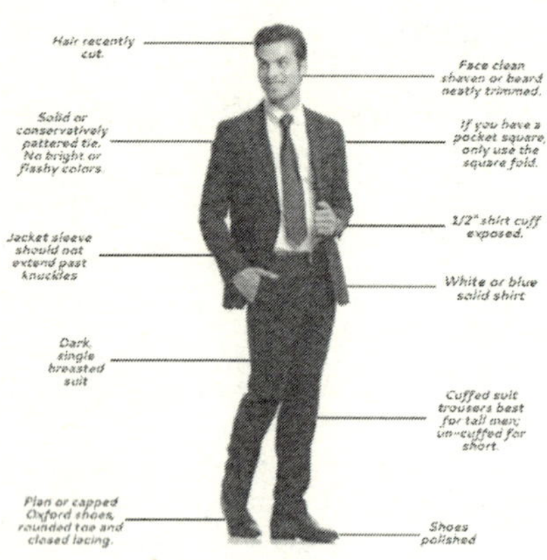

LADIES

Hair
Clean, neat, tidy and elegantly styled

Fingernails
- Clean trimmed fingernails
- Avoid bright or fanciful painted fingernails

Makeup
- Avoid heavy makeup
- Use neutral shades – focus on looking natural and radiant

Perfume
Avoid perfume

Clothes
- Clothes should be wrinkle-free
- Two-piece, matched suit
- Navy, black, grey or dark brown
- Skirt should cover thighs when seated
- Wear clothes that fit

Leather Shoes
No stilettos, flats or platforms

CHAPTER 10

BODY LANGUAGE

Body Language is also known as Non-Verbal Communication, meaning conveying message without speaking. A human mind can think about (approximately) 800 words per minute whereas a human can speak about (approximately) 100 words per minute. Body Language can be defined as the words which have not been spoken but remain in the back of your mind can sometimes get expressed either consciously or subconsciously by means of expressions or gestures or postures.

Understanding body language can be mastered to a large extent, yet not completely, by observing people at various places. Most of the times, I watch movies / people at meetings or malls and tend to grasp quite a lot from them. We need to know the understanding of body language as it helps us to build rapport, get a deal, build relationships, know what is going on in the other person's mind, take decisions, etc. In fact we need body language to live our day-to-day life. Certain important expressions, gestures and postures are what we would know more about in this chapter, with reference to job readiness.

Distance Zone: The distance at which one person stands from the other person differs on certain factors. When we meet someone for the first time we tend to maintain quite some distance (in terms of length). After sometime or a couple of meetings, that distance will reduce and we would be a bit closer than what we were in the first instance. Finally, we would be standing very next to each other, probably, after trust is established (like we know each other for quite some time now).

Just Met Zone

Fig. 6.1

Friendly Zone

Fig. 6.2

Trusted Zone

Fig. 6.3

The best example or Zone would be for each one of us to remember the first day of your college during graduation, as in Fig. 6.1. Day 1, I don't know anyone and anything here. What to do? We would be hesitating to speak with anyone and suddenly there comes someone who introduces and makes you to sit by him/her. Till the first break you would be speaking on a polite manner with maintaining a bit of distance. After the break the formal language will change to addressing personally, by name or nick name, and sitting pretty close to each other, as in Fig. 6.2. By the end of the day it will change completely by pulling ones leg, making fun, and would put our hand on the shoulder of the other person, as in Fig. 6.3.

Handshake: There isn't any defined way to give a handshake. However, certain practices have been observed and followed to make the hand-shake apt and appropriate. While giving a handshake we do need to take care of certain points as our handshake speaks about us. We have different types of handshakes. Most common of them are mentioned below.

Fig. 6.4

The Dominator: These are people who are aggressive and are of dominating nature. These people give their handshake with the palm facing downwards as in Fig. 6.4.

The Submission: These are people who get submissive even with a little authority. They are also gullible with ease as in Fig. 6.5

Fig. 6.5

Fig. 6.6

The Dead Fish: A handshake without energy or squeeze and makes one feel as if they are holding a dead fish. This kind of handshake indicates low self-esteem, as in Fig. 6.6.

The Sweaty Palms: The people who possess sweaty palms are mostly nervous in nature. When they tend to get tensed they, sometimes, precipitate a lot and hence the palms become sweaty as in Fig. 6.7.

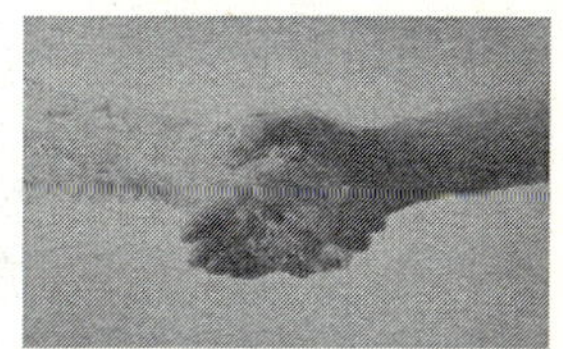

Fig. 6.7

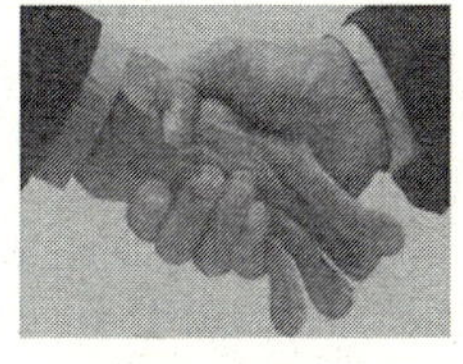

Fig. 6.8

The Hand Crusher: The people who crush the hand of other person until the receiver trembles or writhes in pain are often called as bone crusher or hand crusher. These people do this kind of an act either to bully or threaten the other person or to demonstrate that they are powerful as in Fig. 6.8.

The Queen Finger-Tips: These are people, especially women, who don't like to give a handshake but are forced to do so as in Fig. 6.9. They need to understand that a handshake is an ideal way to socialize and also it is common in the corporate world to give a handshake which helps build rapport and friendship.

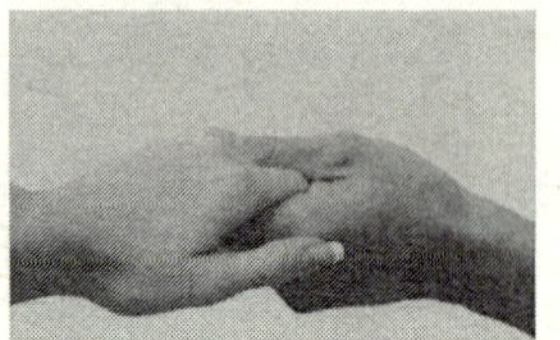

Fig. 6.9

The Hand Hug and The Shug (Shake & Hug): This kind of handshake is seen among politicians and also our near and dear. A regular handshake where the left hand covers the opposite person's right hand is the **Hand Hug**, as in Fig. 6.10. The **Shug** on the other hand is a warm handshake with a hug, as in Fig. 6.11. Both of these handshakes indicate warmness, trustworthy, friendliness and honesty.

Fig. 6.10

Fig. 6.11

Eye Contact: As a child whenever I commit a mistake my mother used to ask me to look into my eyes and tell me the truth. It is pretty easy, with a bit of practice, to read the eyes and identify if someone is telling the truth or concealing any information.

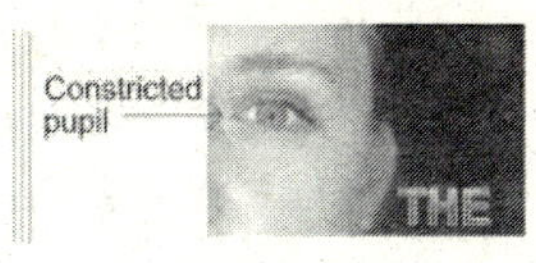

Fig. 6.12

When someone is hiding or concealing any information their pupils become constricted, which are often referred to as beady eyes, and they start sweating with their heart beat increased. They cannot look into the eyes of the other person because of guilt. Hence it is easy to identify if the person is telling the truth, as in Fig. 6.12.

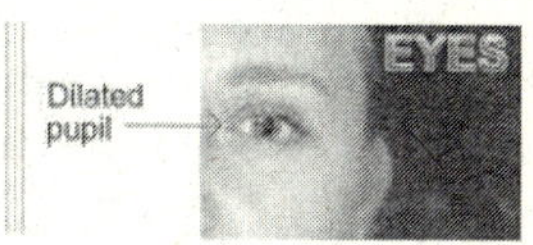

Fig. 6.13

Likewise, if a person is telling the truth, he/she becomes excited and their pupils get dilated. It would be clearly exhibited that the person is eager to share and express. They don't have any hesitation to maintain the eye contact, as in Fig. 6.13.

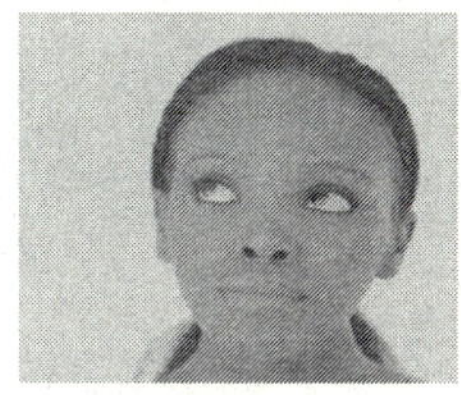
Fig. 6.14

Where to look while answering a question, either during an interview or a meeting? This has been a key question and most of the times there are several contradictory answers to this question. However, it has been established that when answering a question if someone is looking into the roof or in the upward direction, that person is trying to recollect, as in Fig. 6.14.

On the other hand if someone is looking towards the floor or ground indicates that he/she is, ideally, thinking what to tell and how to tell, as in Fig. 6.15.

Fig. 6.15

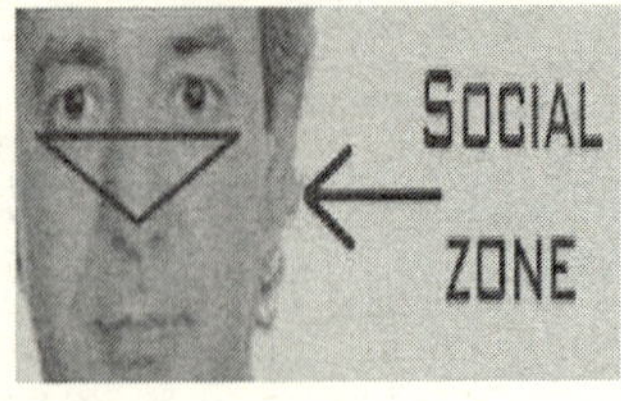

Fig. 6.16

Maintaining eye contact with the opposite gender? Many times people feel uncomfortable to maintain eye contact with the interviewer or superior, especially, if they are of the opposite gender. The simple and easiest way to get rid of this inhibition is by looking at the entire face of the opposite person rather than the eyes. This is not intimidating and people feel quite comfortable as well, as in Fig. 6.16.

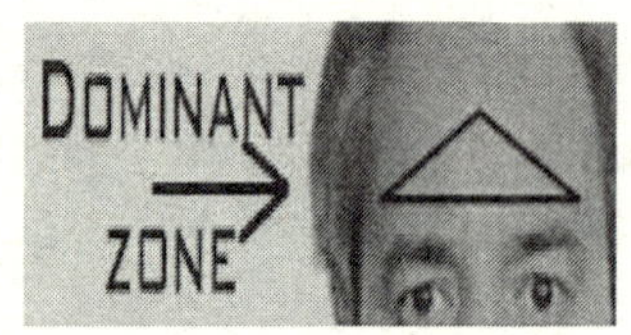

Fig. 6.17

On the other hand, if someone is dominating, intimidating or bullying you try to look at the forehead of that person for about 30 to 40 seconds at least 3 to 4 times. Forehead is considered as the dominant zone and hence you are giving that person a taste of their own medicine. You are intimidating and humiliating them so that they don't do that again to you, as in Fig. 6.17.

Postures and Expressions depict our thoughts as well. However, there are certain postures to be followed to make a positive impact. Mentioned here are some postures that one needs to consider while waiting for interview and during interview as well. Fig. 6.18 and Fig. 6.19 depict the wrong postures used while waiting for the interview. Whereas Fig. 6.20 depicts the correct posture used.

Wrong Postures Used While Waiting For Interview

Fig. 6.18 *Fig. 6.19*

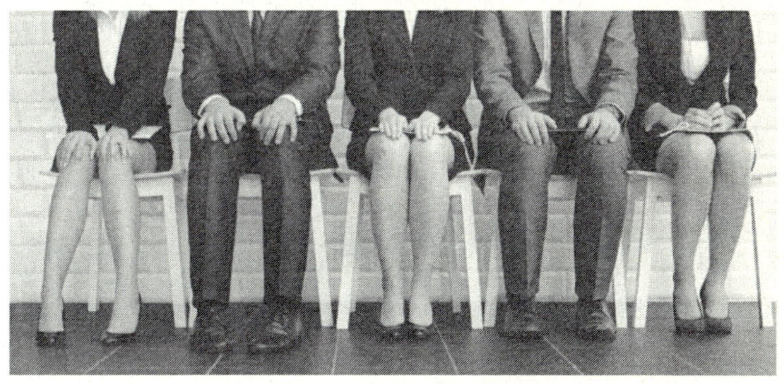

Apt Posture Used While Waiting For Interview

Fig. 6.17

CHAPTER 11

GROUP DISCUSSION

Group discussion can be defined as a group of people facing a similar issue/problem and trying to find a solution for the same. In fact it is a civilized way of discussing and resolving an issue. Group discussion round may be conducted in two ways – Traditional and Non-Traditional. This round is conducted during the interview process to assess the candidate's ability to mingle in a group of people and also to assess his/her language skills such as sentence formation, vocabulary, confidence levels and leadership qualities. It is also believed that this round is used as a mass eliminator.

The best method of preparing for a group discussion is to refer to previous experiences of other candidates or browse the internet for the same. Make a list of the group discussion topics from the said experiences. Gather as many points as possible and also make sure that you have enough examples, statistics to link your points to them. Do your rehearsals either in front of a mirror or with your friends so that you get rid of the nervousness and clear the round with ease.

The traditional way of conducting a group discussion is where the interviewer asks the candidates to speak by adjusting themselves with the flow of the others and also grab opportunities to do so. Mostly there would be two interviewers/evaluators during the group discussion. One would be evaluating the content while the other would be assessing the body language, leadership qualities, initiatives taken, taking control of the discussion and conclude. In this format of group discussion a candidate should make at least 3 attempts to speak.

The non-traditional way of conducting a group discussion is a process where each candidate gets only one chance to speak. In such a situation the candidate should be ready with his/her points to be expressed and ensure that they speak all the points as they would not get another chance to speak.

Dos of Group Discussion	Donts of Group Discussion
➢ Listen to the subject carefully.	➢ Initiate the discussion if you do not have sufficient knowledge about the given topic.
➢ Put down your thoughts on a paper. Let there be at least 35 points on the topic.	➢ Over speak, intervene or snatch other's chance to speak.
➢ Initiate the discussion if you know the subject well.	➢ Argue and shout during the GD as it displays immaturity and uncivilized nature.
➢ Listen to others if you don't know the subject.	➢ Look at the evaluators or a particular group member.
➢ Support you point with some facts and figures.	➢ Talk irrelevant things and distract the discussion.
➢ Make short contribution of 25-30 seconds 3-4 times.	➢ Pose negative body gestures like touching the nose, leaning back on the chair, knocking the table with a pen etc.
➢ Give others a chance to speak.	➢ Mention erratic or unrealistic statistics.
➢ Speak politely and pleasantly. Respect contribution from other members.	➢ Display low self-confidence with shaky voice and trembling hands.
➢ Maintain eye contact with the other group members.	➢ Try to dominate the discussion.
➢ If you cross talk (speak simultaneously with another member of the group, say "I am sorry, you continue and I will speak after you". This gives you a ready-made opportunity to speak after that person.	➢ Put others in an embarrassing situation by asking them to speak if they don't want.
➢ Summarize the discussion if the group has not reached a conclusion.	

CHAPTER 12

RESUME BUILDING AND INTERVIEW SKILLS WITH FAQS

12.1 Resume Building

What is the difference between a Curriculum Vitae (CV) and Résumé?

Curriculum Vitae show cases a detailed presentation of one's academic career and also work experience, if any. On the other hand Résumé is a summary of one's academic career and also work experience.

Primarily, while going for an interview it is important that we need a CV and not a Résumé. Your CV is the first document that is received by the recruiter and hence a lot of care should be taken while preparing it. I, as a trainer, spoke to many HR managers and tried to find out the reason for the rejection of a candidate, especially in the first round itself. The HR personnel have highlighted one major reason behind the rejection and that is candidates, most of the time, don't prepare their CV by themselves rather modify their friends' CV. When a candidate doesn't prepare his/her CV by self, they cannot speak about it and hence they sound that they have faked the information on the CV thus giving an opportunity to the recruiter to reject him / her.

CV should contain genuine information presented in the most attractive way (that doesn't mean one has to decorate it like a bride). It should contain information that is needed by the recruiter to understand your abilities with respect to the job requirement. Mentioned below is a sample of a CV for your benefit.

Certain points to be taken care while preparing your CV are that take a print-out of your CV on an Executive Bond sheet rather than a plain white sheet. It makes one stand-out from the crowd by this kind of presentation. Another point to be noted here is that the languages known has to be in a specific sequence, mother-tongue / native language first. In the sample CV as this person is an Anglo-Indian he mentioned English. All the other languages follow next.

Kevin Kent

6D Jalan Berhala,
Off Jalan Tun Sambanthan,
Kuala Lumpur,
WP Kuala Lumpur – 50470

Phone # +601XXXXXXXX
Email: kevin27jan@gmail.com

Objective

Seeking a challenging position in the field of Linguistic Skills / Soft Skills Training in an organization / institution where I can utilize my skill set for mutual growth and become an asset to the said organization.

Educational Qualification

- ✓ Have achieved First Class Master's Degree in English Literature (M.A. Eng. Lit.) from the University of Toronto, Canada.
- ✓ Have achieved First Class Master's Degree in Business Administration (MBA, Finance) from University of Queensland, Australia.
- ✓ Have achieved First Class Bachelor's Degree in Commerce (B.Com), specialization in Audit and Taxation, from Osmania University, Hyderabad, India.
- ✓ Have achieved First Class Honor's Degree in Arts (B.A.), specialization in Psychology, from Osmania University, Hyderabad, India.

Technical Qualification

- ✓ Have successfully completed, state topper and gold medalist, Type-Writing Higher grade from State Technical Education Board, Hyderabad, India.

Skills

- ✓ Well versed with operating systems like Windows XP/Win 7,8,10
- ✓ MS Office (other than MS Access)
- ✓ Internet Savvy

Training

- ✓ TESOL certification from the American Institute of TESOL.
- ✓ Undergone online training in Bank Secrecy Act (BSA) as per US Federal Law at GECFS.
- ✓ Undergone online training in Anti Money Laundering (AML) as per US Federal Law at GECFS.
- ✓ Undergone Effective Time Management at GECFS.
- ✓ Undergone Voice & Accent Training (American & British Accent) at GECFS & HSBC-HDPI respectively.

Achievements

- ➢ Was awarded a Gold Medal by the Governor of Andhra Pradesh for being the youngest and securing a Distinction in Hindi Pandit exam (at an age of 13 years).
- ➢ Was awarded Gold Medal by the Director of AP State Technical Board for securing highest marks in Type Writing High Speed examination conducted state-wide.
- ➢ Was adjudged as the Best Employee of the Process, "A" Player, Eleven times while at GECFS.

- Was adjudged as the second-best Employee of the Process, "B" Player, Four times while at GECFS.
- Have won QUEST 2006, a quiz championship, while I was working for HSBC.
- Was a member of the team, which won the award of "Best Team of the Quarter" for 2nd and 3rd quarter consecutively at HSBC.

Strengths

- Optimist
- Quick Learner
- Willingness to Learn
- Flexible
- Reliable
- Ability to mingle with anyone, if not everyone, very quickly
- Persuasive
- Garrulous

Weakness

- I used to be a perfectionist. However, I have understood that not all the fingers of a hand are not of the same size, so I have started accepting people as they are and that really helped me to understand them in a much better way.

Hobbies & Interests

- Love to watch Cricket
- To go on Long Drives on motorbike during rain
- Listening to melodious music (preferably English, Hindi, Telugu and Tamil)
- Playing Computer Games (Puzzles, Word Games, etc.)
- Watching Cartoons
- Watching English Movies (preferably Action movies)
- Trying out new dishes / cuisines

Personal Information

Father's Name	:	Late Benjamin Kent
Mother's Name	:	Late Leena Kent
Marital Status	:	Married
Date of Birth	:	27th January, XXXX
Languages Known	:	English, Marwari, Hindi, Telugu, Urdu, Tamil, Kannada, Malayalam, Punjabi & Arabic
Passport #	:	123ABC456

12.2 Interview Skills with FAQs

Interview is also known as Talent Acquisition. The employer/company is in need of manpower with certain skill set/qualities. Hence, I would say that an interview is also "Selling One-self" to the prosperous employer so that they could hire you for their requirement. As a candidate, one should be equipped enough to answer questions from their subject as well as ability to convince the employer that their search ends at him/her.

All/Any interview begins with one "innocent" looking question which is "Tell me about you." "Let us know something more about you." It is pretty important for the candidate to understand as to why is this question asked. This question is asked to understand the abilities of the candidate and also to check his/her skill set with reference to the job requirement and also to amplify certain details that have been mentioned on the CV. The best way to answer this question is to link your positive personality traits/strengths to the job requirement. How can you, as a candidate, justify of being selected for the said role. A detailed explanation of the answer is mentioned the Self-Introduction chapter.

Mentioned below are some of the frequently asked questions (FAQs) during an interview and what could be the best possible

answer to give. However, it is equally important to understand the logic of the interview process. Company needs talented manpower for their needs and as a candidate (both experienced and inexperienced) you need employment. Company needs to verify and amplify certain details that you have mentioned on the CV. If you are aware of this logic it will be pretty easy to answer the questions.

✓ **Tell me about you.**

Refer to chapter on Self-Introduction.

✓ **Why should I/we hire you?**

As a person with adaptable nature, I like to finish my work on time. I am extrovert hence I can mingle with different mentalities of people easily. As a just passed-out graduate I do not possess any work experience but yes, I do have the capability to learn new things quickly and implement them as well. I am sure that my skills would give a better competition to your competitors. Hence I believe that an opportunity will help me prove myself to be an asset to your company.

✓ **What are your strengths and weaknesses?**

Well, my strengths are:

I am a hardworking and flexible person, and take my work very seriously. Also I follow the approach of "make a plan and stick to it". Apart from this I am a very friendly person and adapt easily with people and situations.

Weaknesses: I am a work obsessed person (Workaholic), for me work is everything and I work continuously till the job is done. Now, during the course of working I tend to ignore health and sometimes friends too.

Note: Ensure that you do have sufficient examples to correlate to the strengths as that is the area where most of the people fail. E.g. Flexible person – It was one Sunday while I was working with GECFS where my colleague couldn't come as his father wasn't well and he had to attend him. My team lead called me to extend my shift and she ensured that I will be compensated. To my dismay, I found that three of my colleagues couldn't come that day and I had to do a complete window of the shift i.e. 5 PM to 10 AM. I was completely drained out and I was also compensated with a two day compensatory off. But what was important is that the work didn't suffer and our team was never let down. I was there for the team when it was very important.

These FAQs, which are mentioned below, are for the benefit of youngsters who seek employment. However, a person needs to understand that the answers given are just for the understanding of the process so that they could prepare their own answers.

✓ **Why do you want to work for our company?**

As a just passed-out graduate I am stepping into the corporate world where I would need a platform to exhibit my skills, prove my talent and create my own identity. I want to work in a company like yours because it has a marvelous history of 43 years of being in the IT field and it is a leading company in India and has its branches in 44 countries all over the globe. I believe your company will definitely help me to build my career and as mentioned earlier create an identity for myself.

✓ **How do you feel about working nights and weekends?**

Ideally, I would plan and manage my work in a way which does not require me to work during weekends because I would definitely want to have a balance between professional and personal lives. I believe that this is important in maintaining motivation and high productivity towards work and a positive demeanor at office. However, I understand that there might be demanding times and urgent client/internal requests. In such situations I will definitely make sure to rise up to the occasion and keep up the reputation of the organization.

✓ **Can you work under pressure?**

I believe that it is all a mind game. Make work fun and pressure will never bother anyone. In fact, world's best sprinter **Usain Bolt** has once said that he can give his best once he is under pressure because then he enjoys what he does.

✓ **Are you willing to relocate or travel?**

Sure Sir. I have never been out for studies. So if my company requires me to relocate I will consider it as a boon. Will have a great opportunity to know another culture and provide me an opportunity to learn another language.

✓ **What are your goals?**

My short time goal is to get placed in an organization where I can gain knowledge and where my knowledge is useful to the organization.

My long time goal is to attain respectable position in the organization where I'm working and I should be a good role model to everyone.

✓ **What motivates you to do good job?**

My goal in life is to become a respectful person in the society. I clearly knew the path towards it through highest dedication and hard work to what you do and I am sure it's possible because I have a perfect example i.e. my parents.

✓ **How long would you expect to work for us if hired?**

As a rookie, I would like to work for your company as long as I am able to efficiently contribute to the success and growth of company. I am the kind of person who prefers stability in life. Also, I am really keen to be an instrument in the growth of your company. So I wish to have a long relationship with your company.

✓ **Are you not overqualified for this position?**

I feel myself fortunate enough to get noticed by you this way. However, I don't consider myself "over qualified". In fact, I personally consider this term a relative one. I could be better than the other candidates because of my academics and performance. But I never get satisfied with my efforts and keep learning and experiencing more and more.

The profile that you are offering me in your company is exactly what I have been looking for. So, I would be very ecstatic if I get an opportunity to explore my technical skills in one of the reputed companies such as yours.

✓ **Describe your ideal company, location and job.**

Well, I don't have any specific, company or job as my favorite. However, any place company where I can find an opportunity to utilize my knowledge and skills to the core and grow along with the company. That doesn't restrict with the location. As for the ideal job, I could find this job profile matches with my expectation. That is why I am here now facing this interview and considering it as a step stone.

Note: This is a trap. Before asking this question you may find that the HR personnel becomes quite friendly with you, probably asking you details about your family, life, interests, hobbies, etc. Most of the times candidate are caught unaware of this question and suddenly spill out the name of another company and get rejected in the process.

✓ **What are your career options right now?**

My career option is to be part of one of the most reputed IT companies, as yours, and see myself as one of the most efficient employees.

✓ **Explain how you would be an asset to this organization?**

I am very passionate about my work and always focus on its completion. I do believe in learning in continuation, also from my mistakes. It keeps on making me efficient & perfect bit by bit. Hence I believe that I would be an asset to the organization that I work for.

✓ **Would you lie for the company?**

Firstly, I would try to look for alternatives by which I could avoid lying. If there aren't any then as a matter of ethics of my life, I would excuse myself from the situation where I would have to lie. I would request the management to probably assign the said task to someone else who could accomplish that job.

✓ **Who has inspired you in your life and why?**

I have been inspired by Dr. APJ Abdul Kalam. He, who has changed his life from rags to riches and is a genius by birth and a man of Principles and Ethics. I remember a quote by him which made me motivate many students and unemployed youth i.e. "The problem with India is not Unemployment, in fact it is Unemployability".

✓ **What was the toughest decision you ever had to make?**

Well, the toughest decision that I had to make was whether to join Campus Recruitment Training conducted by my college. The reason was one of the most efficient trainer quit our college and I was not sure if the training programme would be as effective as it was.

✓ **Have you considered starting your own business?**

As I come from a middle class family, I am financially not sound enough to start my own business. Instead of thinking of a business I would as well achieve great heights in the job that I got.

✓ **How do you define success and how do you measure up to your own definition?**

Success is a continuous process of stepping ahead in life where we set a goal and work hard, arise, awake and not stop until we reach that goal. Measurement of success is nothing but achievement/s.

✓ **How much salary do you expect?**

As a novice, I believe that my career is at a bud-blooming stage and at this point money is something but not everything. Hence,

I believe that an organization as reputed as yours would definitely offer a decent and respectable salary.

✓ **Where do you see yourself five years from now?**

In next 5 years I would like to see myself as a key player of this organization, probably a managerial position, with my all abilities and qualities. I'm pretty confident that in the socio technical environment, provided by your esteemed organization, I will achieve that.

✓ **What are your outside interests?**

Spend time with my family, surf the internet to learn new things / technologies, watch television (especially Cartoon Network, Discovery, Animal Planet, National Geographic channels) and to go out with my family on week-ends.

✓ **On a scale of one to ten, rate me as an interviewer.**

As I am a rookie and do not possess any work experience, I don't think that I possess any knowledge or experience to assess/ rate you. All I can say that I have seen both the shades in you i.e. a true professional and a good human being as well.

Note: This is a trap. Never ever rate the interviewer. It shows that you are judgmental and could cost you the job. Be diplomatic and slip away from the situation.

CHAPTER 13

SOFT SKILLS EVALUATION

Questions	Rating 1-Low.....6-High
COMMUNICATION	
1. Tell me about yourself in not more than 2 sentences?	1...2...3...4...5...6
2. As per you, which is more important to you – being a good listener or being a good communicator?	1...2...3...4...5...6
3. Sell me a pen using not more than 5 sentences.	1...2...3...4...5...6
4. How would you explain what do you do for a living to your uncle who is 75 years old?	1...2...3...4...5...6
5. Do you prefer written or verbal communication?	1...2...3...4...5...6
6. If a colleague of yours is demeaning your work achievements, what would you do?	1...2...3...4...5...6
TEAMWORK	
1. Give me some examples of teamwork.	1...2...3...4...5...6
2. Teamwork or Working alone – which one would you prefer and why?	1...2...3...4...5...6
3. Have you had difficulty working with a manager of the opposite gender?	1...2...3...4...5...6
4. Team events – How important are they for you?	1...2...3...4...5...6
5. When your teammates are in agreement on how to tackle a task but you disagree. How would you react?	1...2...3...4...5...6

6. How did you overcome a situation where the team is doing well because the team members aren't getting along?	1…2…3…4…5…6
7. How do you deal with a teammate who isn't taking up the responsibility of doing his/her part of the job?	1…2…3…4…5…6
8. What does team spirit mean to you and what steps would you take to build it?	

LEADERSHIP	
1. When you know that your manager is 100% wrong about something, how would you deal with that situation?	1…2…3…4…5…6
2. What do you expect from a manager?	1…2…3…4…5…6
3. Your teammates started quitting their jobs one after the other. What would you do?	1…2…3…4…5…6
4. If you have to delegate work to a team, what would be your approach?	1…2…3…4…5…6
5. Your company is going through financial crisis and decided to cut down costs, in such a situation what strategy would you take up to fire people?	1…2…3…4…5…6
6. How do you handle disagreements with colleagues?	1…2…3…4…5…6
7. How do you motivate a team?	1…2…3…4…5…6
FLEXIBILITY	
1. What was the most difficult change that you have come across in your career?	1…2…3…4…5…6
2. How do you receive surprises?	1…2…3…4…5…6
3. How did you deal with a short notice request? Give an example.	1…2…3…4…5…6
4. Something unplanned occurred and you may have to rearrange your schedule, how will you deal with it?	1…2…3…4…5…6
5. If you had to learn a new tool at work and start using it on a daily basis, how much time have you taken to learn?	1…2…3…4…5…6

Problem Solving	
1. In your opinion, who makes a good problem solver?	1…2…3…4…5…6
2. Will you sit and work hard to solve a problem or seek suggestions from your colleagues?	1…2…3…4…5…6
3. Give an example of when you have solved a problem.	1…2…3…4…5…6
4. Describe a situation when you had to solve a problem while in crisis.	1…2…3…4…5…6
5. Tell about a situation where you had to analyze information to solve a problem.	1…2…3…4…5…6

Interpersonal Skills	
1. Tell me the ingredients to build good relationship with others.	1…2…3…4…5…6
2. There have been differences between your friend and you which lead to tension between both of you. How did you deal with this situation?	1…2…3…4…5…6
3. Describe a situation where you built good relationship with someone whom you didn't like.	1…2…3…4…5…6
4. Explain how you will convey difficult or unpopular information to someone.	1…2…3…4…5…6
Time Management	
1. Do you take up multi-tasking?	1…2…3…4…5…6
2. Which phrase describes you – "done is better than being perfect" or "everything has to look perfect?"	1…2…3…4…5…6
3. When you have multiple upcoming deadlines, how would prioritize your work?	1…2…3…4…5…6
4. Describe a time when you have struggled to meet deadlines.	1…2…3…4…5…6

5. If your manager assigns you an important and huge task right before the end of the day, how would you reply?	1…2…3…4…5…6
Customer Service	
1. Give an example of how did you deal with an unsatisfied customer.	1…2…3…4…5…6
2. Mention the steps you would take to gain customers' confidence.	1…2…3…4…5…6
3. Give an example where you have gone out of your way or extra mile to satisfy your customer.	1…2…3…4…5…6
4. What was the best customer service that you have ever received?	1…2…3…4…5…6

ABOUT THE AUTHORS

Eashwar N. Rathod is an *Assistant Professor* with *Kalasalingam University* where he conducts training classes for enhancing the employability skills of the students of engineering, business administration and arts & science. He possesses Master's degrees in Business Administration and English Literature from Australia and Canada respectively. He is a TESOL certified soft skills trainer. He is a polyglot with fluency in many languages. With over 25 years of work experience, international and national, in a gamut of fields such as administration, sales, customer service and training in phonetics, voice & accent, communication skills, behavioral skills, problem solving, time management, business communication, etc. He has trained more than 7000 students in professional colleges in Andhra Pradesh, Telangana, Tamil Nadu, Kerala, Karnataka, Rajasthan – domestically, and in Kula Lumpur – internationally. He has been associated with some of the world famous corporate houses such as P&G, Dell, HSBC and GE, to name a few. His passion for teaching has drawn him towards employability skills impartment as it makes the lives of many, especially the students who are from rural regions and who are economically weak.

Prof. Dr. A. Alavudeen is a *Professor and Director Corporate Relations* with *Kalasalingam University*, Krishan Koil, Tamil Nadu. He possesses more than 18 years of teaching experience. He has authored books such as Computer Integrated Manufacturing (PHI), Professional Ethics (Lakshmi Publications), Materials and Metallurgy (Lakshmi Publications) and Fluid Power Control (Charotar). Most of his books have become reference books in famous Indian institutions such as IIST, Anna University, JNTU (Anantapur, Kakinada and Hyderabad), Dr. MGR University, Shivaji University, RGTU, Osmania University, IIIT-D, IIIT-M and IIIT-J. He has done a lot of research in the field of Composite Materials. He has humongous experience in the field of placements and also placement of differently-abled students. He plays a key role in his current role, wherein he places many students into MNCs and core companies. His role ensures that he speaks to many corporate houses for placing our SHIP (speech and hearing impaired) students get either internship offers of job offers as a part of the CSR of a company.